MW01491619

GOD'S CREATIVE POWER®

For Kids

By

Beverly Ann Capps

Copyright

Unless otherwise indicated, all scripture quotations are taken from the King James Version of the Bible.
Scripture quotations marked AMP are taken from the Amplified Bible, Old Testament.
Copyright © 1965, 1987 by Zondervan Corporation
New Testament Copyright © 1958, 1987 by the Lockman Foundation. Used by Permission

God's Creative Power® for Kids
By Beverly Ann Capps
ISBN#978-0-9747513-6-7
Copyright © Beverly Ann Capps

Cover Design by Bush Publishing

Published by
Capps Publishing
PO Box 69
England, AR 72046

Printed in the USA

All rights reserved Under International Copyright Law.
Contents and/or cover may not be reproduced in whole or in part in any form without the express written consent of the Publisher.
®Reigistered in US Patent Office
Gods Creative Power® is a registered US Trademark Permission for use in this book has been granted by Charles Capps.

Forward

The Bible is one of our most important connections to God's will for us.

GOD'S CREATIVE POWER®

God's Word is instruction for what we can be through Christ. God gives us Bible truths to teach us who we are in Him. Through faith in His Word we see God's Word become truth in our lives. Faith is built through accepting the Word of God as fact in our lives and it becomes a reality for us. The truth on which we build our lives is God's Word. God's Word spoken out of our mouth is bringing God's goodness into our life.

CALLING THINGS THAT ARE NOT

God's method is through calling things that be not as though they were. God called Gideon a mighty man of valor when he was hiding behind a winepress. He did not appear to be a "Mighty Man of Valor" at the time but God spoke those words before it came to pass. You must hear and speak these truths before they are true inside of you. We are to be imitators of God, we are created in His image and He spoke things into existence. The same principle operates in us. We speak what we believe and what we believe and speak comes true in our life.

FAITH COMES BY HEARING

ROMANS 10:17 "So then faith cometh by hearing and hearing by the Word of God".

You must realize all the good things that Christ provides for us will only become reality to us when we accept His Word over every circumstance.

While just saying these scriptural truths will not make them reality, saying them is involved in causing faith to come. It is faith in God's Word that will overcome every circumstance. We believe what we hear ourselves say. This is true for both good and bad things. As you begin speaking God's Word over yourself, you will start believing that God's Word is working for you. Make sure the words you are speaking at all times are in line with Jesus' words!

We have provided these confessions for you so you can build spiritual truths in your life. You will eventually be able to quote the confessions from memory you will be amazed at how quickly you begin to believe what God has said about you in His Word.

Start speaking God's Word today and you will be building up your faith in God's Word and believe good things about yourself.

Beverly Ann Capps

Contents

AUTHORITY	7
FAITH	9
COMFORT	11
SAFETY	13
OVERCOMING WORRY	15
OBEDIENCE	17
WISDOM	19
HEALING	21
SALVATION	23
PEACE	25
POWER OF GOD'S WORD	27
GOD'S GIFTS	29
PROVISION	31
GUIDANCE	33
GENEROSITY	35
ABUNDANCE	37
GOD'S GOODNESS	39
GOD'S ABILITY	41
GOD'S LOVE	43
KINDNESS AND SERENITY	45
TRUST	47
HONESTY	49
BLESSING	51
SALVATION PRAYER	53

SCRIPTURE

Romans 12:21

Be not overcome of evil, but overcome evil with good.

AUTHORITY

I am one with Christ and Satan
has no power over me. I win over
evil by doing and speaking good
things.

SCRIPTURE

I John 4:4

Ye are of God, little children, and have overcome them: because greater is he that is in you, than he that is in the world.

FAITH

I am of God and will overcome
Satan for God is greater inside
of me than Satan who is in the
world.

SCRIPTURE

Psalms 23:1-6

A psalm of David

The Lord is my shepherd; I shall not want. He maketh me to lie down in green pastures: he leadeth me beside the still waters. He restoreth my soul; he leadeth me in the paths of righteousness for his name's sake. Yea, though I walk through the valley of the shadow of death, I will fear no evil: for thou art with me; thy rod and thy staff they comfort me. Thou preparest a table before me in the presence of mine enemies: thou anointest my head with oil; my cup runneth over. Surely goodness and mercy shall follow me all the days of my life: and I will dwell in the house of the Lord forever.

COMFORT

I will not fear evil, for Jesus is with me, and His Word, and his spirit they comfort me. God will always protect me.

SCRIPTURE

Isaiah 54:17

No weapon that is formed against thee shall prosper; and every tongue that shall rise against thee in judgment thou shalt condemn. This is the heritage of the servants of the Lord, and their righteousness is of me, saith the Lord.

Psalms 1:1-3

Blessed is the man that walketh not in the counsel of the ungodly, nor standeth in the way of sinners, nor sitteth in the seat of the scornful. But his delight is in the law of the Lord; and in his law doth he meditate day and night. And he shall be like a tree planted by the rivers of water, that bringeth forth his fruit in his season; his leaf also shall not wither; and whatsoever he doeth shall prosper.

SAFETY

Nothing bad that comes against me will win for my righteousness is of Jesus. Whatever I do will work out well.

SCRIPTURE

Psalm 91:10-11

There shall no evil befall thee, neither shall any plague come nigh thy dwelling. For he shall give his angels charge over thee, to keep thee in all thy ways.

Proverbs 12:28

In the way of righteousness is life; and in the pathway thereof there is no death.

I John 5:4-5

For whatsoever is born of God overcometh the world: and this is the victory that overcometh the world, even our faith. Who is he that overcometh the world, but he that believeth that Jesus is the Son of God?

I John 4:4

Ye are of God, little children, and have overcome them: because greater is he that is in you than he that is in the world.

OVERCOMING WORRY

Nothing bad will happen to me
or my family for God's angels
watch over me and take care of
me wherever I go.

I am born of God and I have world
overcoming faith residing on the
inside of me. For greater is He
that is in me, than he that is in the
world.

SCRIPTURE

James 1:22

But be ye doers of the word, and not hearers only, deceiving your own selves.

OBEDIENCE

I do what God's Word says, and I am blessed in what I do. I am happy because I do God's Word. God's Word abides inside of me.

SCRIPTURE

Psalms 138:8

The Lord will perfect that which concerneth me: thy mercy, O Lord, endureth for ever: forsake not the works of thine own hands.

Colossians 3:16

Let the word of Christ dwell in you richly in all wisdom; teaching and admonishing one another in psalms and hymns and spiritual songs, singing with grace in your hearts to the Lord.

WISDOM

I let the word of Christ dwell in me richly in all wisdom.

I use my faith to stop every bad thing   that comes against me. When faith is present, fear must leave.

The Lord will perfect that which concerneth me.

SCRIPTURE

Galatians 3:13

Christ hath redeemed us from the curse of the law, being made a curse for us: for it is written, Cursed is every one that hangs on a tree.

Romans 8:11

But if the Spirit of him that raised up Jesus from the dead dwell in you, he that raised up Christ from the dead shall also quicken your mortal bodies by his Spirit that dwelleth in you.

HEALING

Jesus has redeemed me from every bad thing. I will not let any sickness come to live in my body. Every germ and virus that tries to make me sick, dies instantly in the name of Jesus. Every part of my body works the way God made it to work.

SCRIPTURE

Romans 10:9-11

That if thou shalt confess with thy mouth the Lord Jesus, and shalt believe in thine heart that God hath raised him from the dead, thou shalt be saved. For with the heart man believeth unto righteousness; and with the mouth confession is made unto salvation. For the scripture saith, Whosoever believeth on him shall not be ashamed.

Romans 5:17

For if by one man's offence death reigned by one; much more they which receive abundance of grace and of the gift of righteousness shall reign in life by one, Jesus Christ.

SALVATION

I always win over bad things
because Jesus died for me and
I confess Him as my Lord and
Savior. God lives inside of me.

And I, having received the gift of
righteousness do reign as a king in
life by Jesus Christ.

SCRIPTURE

Colossians 3:15

And let the peace of God rule in your hearts, to the which also ye are called in one body; and be ye thankful.

Philippians 4:6-9

Be careful for nothing; but in every thing by prayer and supplication with thanksgiving let your requests be made known unto God. And the peace of God, which passeth all understanding, shall keep your hearts and minds through Christ Jesus. Finally, brethren, whatsoever things are true, whatsoever things are honest, whatsoever things are just, whatsoever things are pure, whatsoever things are lovely, whatsoever things are of good report; if there be any virtue, and if there be any praise, think on these things. Those things which ye have both learned, and received, and heard, and seen in me, do: and the God of peace shall be with you.

PEACE

I let the peace of God rule in my
heart and I refuse to worry about
anything.

I do what God says in His Word
and I do not listen to bad things
in Jesus Name. Whatever is good,
perfect, lovely, and of good report,
I think on these things. I am in
perfect peace.

SCRIPTURE

Psalms119:89

For ever, O Lord, thy word is settled in heaven.

Isaiah 54:13

And all thy children shall be taught of the Lord; and great shall be the peace of thy children.

POWER OF GOD'S WORD

The Bible is full of power from heaven and I speak His Word on the earth.

Great is my peace because I know Jesus.

SCRIPTURE

Galatians 3:13-14

Christ hath redeemed us from the curse of the law, being made a curse for us: for it is written, Cursed is every one that hangeth on a tree: That the blessing of Abraham might come on the Gentiles through Jesus Christ; that we might receive the promise of the Spirit through faith.

Deuteronomy 28:1-2

And it shall come to pass, if thou shalt hearken diligently unto the voice of the Lord thy God, to observe and to do all his commandments which I command thee this day, that the Lord thy God will set thee on high above all nations of the earth: And all these blessings shall come on thee, and overtake thee, if thou shalt hearken unto the voice of the Lord thy God.

GOD'S GIFTS

Christ takes care of me…I am blessed.

Jesus has saved me from not having enough of what I need. He makes my body well and has given me life.

SCRIPTURE

Proverbs 3:5

Trust in the Lord with all thine heart; and lean not unto thine own understanding.

II Corinthians 8:9

For ye know the grace of our Lord Jesus Christ, that, though he was rich, yet for your sakes he became poor, that ye through his poverty might be rich.

PROVISION

I trust in the Lord with all my
heart and I lean not to my own
understanding.

I am not poor because he supplies
all my needs, I am not sick because
he makes me well, he has given
me eternal life. The Word of God
is true in my life.

SCRIPTURE

John 10:4-5

And when he putteth forth his own sheep, he goeth before them, and the sheep follow him: for they know his voice. And a stranger will they not follow, but will flee from him: for they know not the voice of strangers.

Psalms 37:3-6

Trust in the Lord and do good; so shalt thou dwell in the land, and verily thou shalt be fed. Delight thyself also in the Lord; and he shall give thee the desires of thine heart. Commit thy way unto the Lord; trust also in him; and he shall bring it to pass. And he shall bring forth thy righteousness as the light and thy judgment as the noonday.

GUIDANCE

I do follow the Good Shepherd and
I know His voice and the voice of
a stranger I will not follow.

When I put God first he gives me
the desires of my heart.

SCRIPTURE

Luke 6:38

Give, and it shall be given unto you; good measure, pressed down, and shaken together, and running over, shall men give into your bosom. For with the same measure that ye mete withal it shall be measured to you again.

GENEROSITY

I give to others and it is given back unto me.

No matter how much I give, it is given back to me, I am happy to give and God gives me all that I need so I can do good.

SCRIPTURE

Isaiah 53:5-6

But he was wounded for our transgressions, he was bruised for our iniquities: the chastisement of our peace was upon him and with his stripes we are healed. All we like sheep have gone astray; we have turned every one to his own way; and the Lord hath laid on him the iniquity of us all.

II Corinthians 8:9

For ye know the grace of our Lord Jesus Christ, that though he was rich, yet for your sakes he became poor, that ye through his poverty might be rich.

John 5:24

Verily, Verily, I say unto you, He that heareth my word, and believeth on him that sent me, hath everlasting life, and shall not come into condemnation; but is passed from death unto life.

Philippians 4:19

But my God shall supply all your need according to his riches in glory by Christ Jesus.

ABUNDANCE

There is no lack for my God supplieth all of my need according to His riches in glory by Christ Jesus.

For poverty He has given me wealth, for sickness He has given me health, for death He has given me eternal life.

I don't have any needs that God will not take care of because Jesus died for me. I have abundance in my life and no lack.

SCRIPTURE

John 10:10

The thief cometh not, but for to steal, and to kill, and to destroy: I am come that they might have life, and that they might have it more abundantly.

John 10:4-5

And when he putteth forth his own sheep, he goeth before them, and the sheep follow him: for they know his voice. And a stranger will they not follow, but will flee from him: for they know not the voice of strangers.

GOD'S GOODNESS

Jesus came to earth so that I can
have a good life full of good things.
I hear God's voice and the voice
of a stranger I will not follow.

SCRIPTURE

Philippians 4:13

I can do all things through Christ which strengtheneth me.

Psalms 27:1

The Lord is my light and my salvation; whom shall I fear? The Lord is the strength of my life; of whom shall I be afraid?

Nehemiah 8:10b

for the joy of the Lord is your strength.

James 1:5

If any of you lack wisdom, let him ask of God, that giveth to all men liberally, and upbraideth not; and it shall be given him.

GOD'S ABILITY

I am filled with the knowledge of the Lord's will in all wisdom and spiritual understanding.

The joy of the Lord is my strength. The Lord is the strength of my life.

The Spirit of truth abideth in me and teaches me all things, and He guides me into all truth. Therefore, I confess I have perfect knowledge of every situation and every circumstance that I come up against. For I have the wisdom of God.

Because Jesus is in my life I have His power in me. There is nothing that I cannot do through Christ.

SCRIPTURE

Psalm 35:27

Let them shout for joy, and be glad, that favour my righteous cause: yea, let them say continually, Let the Lord be magnified, which hath pleasure in the prosperity of his servant.

Ephesians 3:14-21

For this cause I bow my knees unto the Father of our Lord Jesus Christ. Of whom the whole family in heaven and earth is named. That he would grant you, according to the riches of his glory to be strengthened with might by his Spirit in the inner man; That Christ may dwell in your hearts by faith; that ye being rooted and grounded in love, May be able to comprehend with all saints what is the breadth, and length, and depth, and height; And to know the love of Christ, which passeth knowledge, that ye might be filled with all the fullness of God. Now unto him that is able to do exceeding abundantly above all that we ask or think, according to the power that worketh in us. Unto him be glory in the church by Christ Jesus through out all ages, world without end. Amen

GOD'S LOVE

The Lord is happy with me and
I am blessed in everything that I
do. Everything works out well for
me. I am strehgthened by God's
spirit.

SCRIPTURE

Ephesians 4:29-32

Let no corrupt communication proceed out of your mouth, but that which is good to the use of edifying, that it may minister grace unto the hearers. And grieve not the holy Spirit of God, whereby ye are sealed unto the day of redemption. Let all bitterness, and wrath, and anger and clamour, and evil speaking, be put away from you, with all malice. And be ye kind one to another, tender hearted, forgiving one another, even as God for Christ's sake hath forgiven you.

I Corinthians 2:16

For who hath known the mind of the Lord, that he may instruct him: But we have the mind of Christ.

KINDNESS AND SERENITY

I have good friends because I am a good friend to others.

I remember what I learn because I have the mind of Christ.

I am not nervous about my school work   or tests because I have perfect peace.

SCRIPTURE

Proverbs 3:1-5

My son, forget not my law; but let thine heart keep my commandments: for length of days, and long life, and peace, shall they add to thee. Let not mercy and truth forsake thee: bind them about thy neck; write them upon the tablet of thine heart: So shalt thou find favour and good understanding in the sight of God and man. Trust in the Lord with all thine heart; and lean not unto thine own understanding.

TRUST

My mind is at peace because of
Christ in me.

I can do all things through Christ's
ability inside of me.

I am obedient and respectful to
my parents and my teachers, and
I have favor with them.

SCRIPTURE

Ephesians 4:15

But speaking the truth in love, may grow up into him in all things, which is the head, even Christ.

I Corinthians 13:6

Rejoiceth not in iniquity, but rejoiceth in the truth.

HONESTY

I speak the truth of the Word of God in love and I grow up into the Lord Jesus Christ in all things.

I speak the truth because the truth is in me and I do not deceive others.

SCRIPTURE

James 1:22

But be ye doers of the word, and not hearers only, deceiving your own selves.

Ephesians 6:1-4

Children, obey your parents in the Lord: for this is right. Honour thy father and mother; (which is the first commandment with promise;) That it may be well with thee, and thou mayest live long on the earth. And, ye fathers, provoke not your children to wrath: but bring them up in the nurture and admonition of the Lord.

Isaiah 1:19

If ye be willing and obedient, ye shall eat the good of the land.

Isaiah 54:17

No weapon that is formed against thee shall prosper; and every tongue that shall rise against thee in judgment thou shalt condemn. This is the heritage of the servants of the Lord, and their righteousness is of me, saith the Lord.

BLESSING

I am a doer of the Word of God, and am blessed in my deeds. I am happy in those things which I do because I am a doer of the Word of God.

I am blessed in all that I do because I am obedient to Christ.

No weapon formed against me shall prosper, for my righteousness is of the Lord. But whatever I do will prosper for I'm like a tree that's planted by the rivers of water.

SALVATION PRAYER

Dear God, You loved the world so much, You gave Your only begotten Son to die for our sins so that whoever believes in Him will not perish, but have eternal life (John 3:16). Your Word says that if I confess with my mouth and believe in my heart, I shall be saved, or born again (Romans 10:9-10). The Bible says we are saved by grace through faith as a gift from You. There is nothing I can do to earn salvation. I now confess Jesus as my Lord and Savior. Lord Jesus, I ask You to come into my heart and forgive me of my sins. I believe in my heart that You God raised Jesus from the dead so that I could be saved.

Thank You, Jesus for saving me. I am so grateful!

In Jesus' Name, Amen!

BOOKS BY BEVERLY CAPPS

THE THREE BEARS IN THE MINISTRY
THE THREE LITTLE PIGS
LITTLE RED RIDINGHOOD
LITTLE RED HEN
JACK AND THE BEANSTALK
CHICKEN LITTLE CONQUERS FEAR
SEEDTIME STORIES
HOW CAN I PLEASE YOU, GOD?
PRAYERS FOR PRE-SCHOOLERS
SHADRACH, MESHACH AND ABEDNEGO
DANIEL AND THE LIONS' DEN

GOD, ARE YOU REALLY REAL?
GOD IS MY BEST FRIEND
GOD IS NEVER TOO BUSY TO LISTEN
GOD LOVES MY TEDDY BEAR, TOO!
GOD HAS ALL THE ANSWERS
IS EASTER JUST FOR BUNNIES?

GOD'S CREATIVE POWER FOR BABIES AND TODDLERS
GOD'S CREATIVE POWER FOR PRESCHOOLERS
GOD'S CREATIVE POWER FOR KIDS
GOD'S CREATIVE POWER FOR GRANDPARENTs

VISIT US @ FAITHTALES.COM
1-800-388-5437
BEVERLY CAPPS MINISTRIES
BOX 69
ENGLAND, ARKANSAS 72046

Sunday School
Curriculum for Babies

Jesus Loves Me!

0 –12 Months

A complete year of lessons that minister to babies!

Organized and easy to use—even for the *first-time* teacher!

This set includes a sample of nursery policies and standards to use as a guide for organizing a church nursery. Help babies learn to recognize the Bible and Jesus. Teach them to recognize how much Jesus loves them! Fill the air around little ones with the love of God and His Word, planting an everlasting seed of faith! Flexible—begin *anytime!*

THIS SET INCLUDES:

- Master Lesson Book
- Teachers Instruction CD
- A Lullaby CD
- Poster of Jesus
- Baby Praise Book
- Master Set Reproducible Take-Home Papers
- One Bible
- Sample of Nursery Policies for Organization
- Two Children's Story Books by Beverly Capps:
    - Prayers for Preschoolers
    - How Can I Please You God?

$199.00

Samples available! See order form.

Sunday School
Curriculum for Toddlers

Jesus Loves Me, Too!

Toddlers from 12–24 Months

A complete year of lessons for toddlers.

This curriculum promotes the foundation of the authority of God's Word to change lives, while focusing on Jesus Christ and our love for Him! Included is a **full-bodied**, stuffed, white bunny puppet that can be used to help toddlers learn to sing praise songs. The lovable bunny keeps interest alive! Toddlers will develop a new awareness of Jesus and His goodness and will grow spiritually by the confession of God's Word over them!

THIS SET INCLUDES:

- Master Lesson Book
- Teacher's Instruction CD
- Full Bodied Stuffed Bunny Puppet
- Two Story Books by Beverly Capps:
    - Prayers for Preschoolers
    - How Can I Please You God?
- Poster of Jesus
- Baby Praise Book and CD
- Master Set Reproducible Take-Home Papers
- One Bible

$199.00   Samples available! See order form.

order online at WWW.FAITHTALES.COM

Preschool
Curriculum for Ages 2-5

Friends With God

Preschoolers Ages 2-5

17 weeks of lessons

Organized and easy to use—even for the first-time teacher!

Having a relationship with God is important for children. This planned-and-organized curriculum is part of a series of teachings that will help children learn how to have a close trust in Him. It is provided to help teachers train preschoolers to know that God is their best friend and that He always will listen to them. In fact, He looks forward to it! *Nothing else to buy! You can start anytime during the year.*

THIS SET INCLUDES:

- 17 Week Master Lesson Book
- Teacher's Instruction CD
- No-Mess Creative Wikki-Stix (two packages)
- "Gladly the Bear" Puppet
- Two Sheets Flannel Graph Characters
- Reproducible Coloring Sheets/Master Copies
- Three books:
    - God Is Never Too Busy To Listen
    - The Three Bears in the Ministry
    - Little Red Ridinghood (retold as a faith tale)

$169.00   Samples available! See order form.

Preschool

Curriculum for Ages 2-5

God's Word is Truth

Preschoolers Ages 2-5

17 weeks of lessons

Organized and easy to use—even for the first-time teacher!

This organized and easy-to-use curriculum is part of a series of teachings that will help children build a relationship with God. It is provided to help teachers train preschoolers to know that God's Word is always truth, regardless of what might be going on around them! Having confidence enough to believe and rely on God's Word proves that a child has advanced his or her faith, and has strengthened his or her relationsip with God. *You can get started teaching preschoolers today with God's Word is Truth!*

THIS SET INCLUDES:

* 17 Week Master Lesson Book
* Teacher's Instruction CD
* No-Mess Creative Wikki-Stix (two packages)
* Coloring Sheets for Handout (reproducible)
* Duck Puppet (full size and soft)
* Two Sheets Flannel Graph Characters
* Three books:
    God, Are You Really Real?
    Jack and the Beanstalk (retold as a faith tale)
    Little Red Hen (retold as a faith tale)

$169.00   Samples available! See order form.

Preschool

Curriculum for Ages 2-5

Obedience and Forgiveness

Preschoolers Ages 2-5

17 weeks of lessons

Organized and easy to use—even for the first-time teacher!

Preschool children are not too young to learn how to have a good relationship with God. This good relationship depends on teaching them Bible stories, Bible principles, and elements of relationship. This package is designed to teach preschoolers about obedience and forgiveness. *Everything you need to get started teaching preschoolers at anytime during the year.*

THIS SET INCLUDES:

- 17 Week Master Lesson Book
- Teacher's Instruction CD
- No-Mess Creative Wikki-Stix (two packages)
- Coloring Sheets for Handout (reproducible)
- Benji Bunny Puppet
- 2 Sheets of Flannel Graph Characters
- Three books:
  Chicken Little Conquers Fear
  The Three Little Pigs
     (Building Your House Upon a Rock)
  God Is My Best Friend

$169.00   Samples available! See order form.

Faith Building
Curriculum for Ages 6-12

Mighty Through God

Children Ages 6-12

17 weeks of lessons

Understanding God's power teaches children to have reverent fear of Almighty God; or in other words, understanding His power is key to their having respect for Him. To help build this kind of reverance toward God, this curriculum helps children learn the character of God by studying the names of God. When children know God's character, they build a closer relationship with Him.

Children involved in this curriculum will also study Bible stories of men of God and how they related to Him. Through these stories, children will learn about God's awesome power and His ability to work on our behalf. Children will learn that He is our loving Father, but He is also Almighty God, Jehovah!

This faith-building curriculum is organized and easy to use, regardless of the teacher's level of experience.

Children will learn the names of the books of the New Testament, all in order by the end of the this curriculum. You can start any time of the year.

THIS SET INCLUDES:

* 17 Week Master Lesson Book
* Master Set of Reproducible Activity Sheets
* Master Set of Reproducible Coloring Sheets
* Two Books:
    Daniel and the Lions' Den
    Seedtime Stories

$137.50   Samples available! See order form.

order online at WWW.FAITHTALES.COM